PASSPORT TO GROWTH

Leadership Lessons From an Expat

Patricia East

Copyright © 2024 Patricia East

Published by WeBook Publishing – Los Angeles, CA
All rights in the English language reserved.

No portion of this book may be copied, stored in recovery systems, or transferred by any means, whether electronic or mechanical, nor photocopied, recorded, or otherwise, without the author's and the Publisher's written permission.

This is a work of nonfiction based on the author's experiences adapting to a new country, language, culture, and life. For information, please email info@webookpublishing.com

First Edition

ISBN: 979-89886684-5-9
LCCN: 2024908690
Written by Patricia East
Copy Editing: Ana Silvani
Assistant Editor: Maria Acero
Cover Art: Yale East
Clipart by Freepik
Interior Formatting: Sazzarul Islam
Manufactured in the United States of America

Note:

Much care and technique were employed in editing this book. However, there can be no assurance that it will be free of minor typing errors, printing issues, or even conceptual ambivalence. In any such case, we ask that the issue be notified to our customer service at the e-mail address info@webookpublishing.com

PASSPORT TO GROWTH

Leadership Lessons From an Expat

Patricia East

In loving memory of my parents,

Sonia Regina Fernandes Coelho (Soninha; Gina; Madame) & José Augusto Enes Coelho (Zé do Fubaca; Guto; Dario). This book is a tribute to their legacy and the immeasurable impact they had in shaping who I am today.

To my loving husband, Yale East, for the unwavering support, constant encouragement, and precious contribution to make this book come to life;

To my mentor, Larissa Rinaldi, for the guidance that helped make this dream come to fruition;

To all my family, especially my siblings and niece, Manu, who is our bright shining light.

CONTENTS

About This Book 2
Introduction 4
1: A Lifelong Learning Journey 8
2: The Middle Child Syndrome? 16
3: How Hr Found Me 24
4: The Blogger 36
5: Being Authentic 44
6: Life In The Silicon Valley 50
7: I Speak Funny 56
8: Squeezing Into A Box 64
9: An Optimist With A Plan B 70
10: All You Need Is Love 74
Epilogue 88
About The Author 92

ABOUT THIS BOOK

This book is a unique blend of personal memoir, the chronicle of my journey as an expat along with valuable lessons that can benefit fellow expatriates. These stories are based on my memories and are as accurate as my recollection permits.

As you embark on this journey, I encourage you to contemplate your own experiences and invite you to consider what lessons can be applied to your own personal growth.

INTRODUCTION

Passport to Growth

"You have to leave the island to see the island," wrote José Saramago in 1997. That was also the year I came to the USA for the very first time as a teenager on a family vacation. Being in a different country and having to speak another language sparked my adventurous spirit. At that time, I felt I *needed* to live abroad. For the next several years, I considered student exchange programs in countries like the US, Australia, Spain, and South Africa. The ideas were always flowing, but none of them seemed financially doable. However, during my last year in university, I stumbled upon something called "Au Pair in America." I had no idea what that was, but as I delved deeper, I realized I checked all the boxes: I had half-decent English skills, enjoyed taking care of kids, wanted to study, and yes, enjoyed earning some money, too. I signed up for the program, and several months later, there I was, landing in the USA for a one-year adventure. Luckily, I "won the au pair lottery" and was matched with a fantastic family with two kids who warmly welcomed me as one of their own. I spent a year living with them in a small town in Connecticut, where I learned a great deal and significantly improved my English skills.

After my Au Pair year and upon returning to Brazil, I experienced a cultural shock. I had changed so much in one year, while it seemed like people around me had frozen in time: they were in the same place, doing the same things, living the same old life. And once again, I started considering how to move back to the US.

Even though it was still unclear to me what I would do or how I would do it, I knew that focusing on my career was crucial, and I didn't want to work in fields not aligned with my education. I explored several different options, but nothing felt like the right thing or the right time. Overtime, the dream moved to the side of my daily routine.

Several years later, and still living in Brazil, that dream seemed distant. I was no longer considering moving to the U.S., not because I didn't want it anymore but because it seemed almost impossible.

So, there I was, working for an American company for a couple of years, when I unexpectedly saw an opening in the HR department at the company's headquarters in San Francisco, CA. Without hesitation, I wrote an e-mail to my then-boss, the Chief Finance Officer, expressing my interest. I had many selling points, including my track record with the company, my commitment and loyalty, and my previous experience living in the U.S.

At that moment, a sense of extreme confidence washed over me, and I thought, *I got this*. I was so naïve to believe that my Au Pair year in Connecticut, living with a host family who provided everything, from food to cell phone and even a brand-new fancy car, had prepared me for the challenges I would face when I moved across the globe on my own. It's true what they say – ignorance truly is bliss.

I soon discovered that building credit history in the U.S. and assembling Ikea furniture were just the tip of the iceberg. There was so much more for me to learn, not only about this new place but, most importantly, about myself.

1

A LIFELONG LEARNING JOURNEY

―∞―

*I have no special talent.
I am only passionately
curious.*

-Albert Einstein

My favorite Pixar animation film is probably *Inside Out*. I have always loved the brain, so I was fascinated to learn the story inside the mind of Riley, an 11-year-old girl. In the film, we learn about Riley's core memories, which are those pivotal moments in her experience that have significant emotional weight and contribute to shaping her personality and identity.

Reflecting on my own experiences, I believe that one of my core memories – certainly not the first one, but maybe the oldest one I remember – is when I started attending school. I have a sister who is two years older than me. At that time, we didn't have other siblings, and our mom was a stay-at-home mom. At the age of 4, my sister started going to preschool. I remember seeing the school bus full of kids stopping in front of the house every day to pick her up. I watched from the living room window. I cried almost daily because I also wanted to go to school. I guess that in my mind, if all those kids on the bus are happy and are going to school, the school must be a fun place. I want to go there. And I cried some more. Every. Single. Day. Rinse and Repeat. Eventually, my mom gave in. I was only two and a half years old, and she decided to put me in school because, poor thing, she was probably tired of me crying all the time, saying that I wanted to go to school.

In school, I felt important and like a "big girl" who now had a school uniform and went to this special place like the older kids. I played and learned a few things, but at that age, I think I mostly played. And I believe that's the core memory I created: school is a fun place, and I love it.

When my sister went to first grade, I wanted to learn all the things she was learning. I wanted to read and write. But she was a little controlling and only allowed me to look at her books until a specific page, "This is only for first graders; you are not supposed to learn this yet." I didn't care. I still skimmed through her books and her homework and wanted to read everything she was reading.

In kindergarten, I was already more advanced than other kids (thank you, sis), so I took a test to join this other class, which was some sort of in-between kindergarten and first grade. I remember being very nervous during the test, which mostly consisted of writing cursive letters repeatedly. There was probably more in this test, but all I remember is how difficult it was to write several consecutive cursive j's and s's on the page. And I did it. I passed the test, and off I went to this "special class."

Over the years, school always felt reasonably easy, so I never put much effort into being an A+ student. In fact, in Brazil, we don't measure academic progress with GPA scores, so I didn't feel very incentivized to be the A+ type of student. I was a good enough student, but I had various interests and many after-school activities. Plus, I always made the effort to find plenty of time to hang out with my friends.

After high school, I started having some reality checks. First was the challenge of passing the university admission exam, which we call *vestibular*[1]. After finishing high school, I took one year to study for admission tests in a specific

---

[1] *Vestibular* is an entry exam for colleges and universities and probably the most dreadful word for most high school students.

year-long course. All the high school content and some more were reviewed to prepare students to take different admission tests for different universities. The *vestibular* for the top universities is always very competitive, and the tests are very difficult. But I also learned that an easy test is not a good thing. If it's easy for me, it's easy for everyone else, so if you make one silly mistake on just one question, it can cost you the next four to five years of your life. As much as I liked to study and was learning a lot of exciting things about biology and organic chemistry, I would describe that year as *hell*. Not only did I have to study all the other subjects I didn't like, including physics and calculus, but the pressure was very high. People were not there because they enjoyed learning or wanted to make new friends but because we were all feeling the stress, anxiety, and the weight of doing well on all those tests.

I did okay. I ended up going to a private college, which was my second option. My first one would have been to study Occupational Therapy at a public university. Looking back, I am grateful I didn't pass that test. I think having a degree in Psychology opened many more doors for me.

In university, I rediscovered the pleasure of studying. I joined study groups, conducted research, served as tutor at a psychology lab, and I loved the brain so much that I even memorized the dictionary of psychopharmacology. *Why?* (note: I don't remember most of what I learned in psychopharmacology, but it turned me into a nerd during my college years who was afraid of experimenting with any substance. Ha!).

As the years go by, I occasionally feel the itch to go back to school. There is something very special to me about being in an academic environment. I crave all the possibilities and knowledge to be uncovered.

There is a popular belief that the best way to learn is by teaching. Currently, I am delighted to be involved in mentoring low-income Brazilian students who are learning English as a second language (ESL). Teaching requires creativity, adaptability, and patience. It also helps me to reinforce what I have learned from my days studying ESL.

I'm consistently impressed by these students' dedication and perseverance. These kids have learned from a young age that success requires hard work and determination. They earned scholarships to attend private schools, they have mentors like me to teach them ESL, and they don't take these opportunities for granted. Their resourcefulness teaches me every day the power of humility, resilience, and growth mindset.

Since I mentioned the growth mindset in the previous paragraph, I want to add a few thoughts about this topic. First and foremost, I am glad to see a surge in discussions about applying a **growth mindset** in the corporate world. Carol Dweck[2]'s remarkable research has left the classroom. Finally, we are discussing how a growth mindset can impact an individual's performance and management style as well as organizational success.

---

[2] Dweck, C. S. (2006). Mindset: the new psychology of success. Ballantine.

However, when talking about the growth mindset, we need to address the elephant in the room because I've seen many misconceptions about this theme. One of the biggest being the belief that a growth mindset is solely about growing a business or a career in terms of numbers and prestigious job titles. This oversimplification leads to erroneous assumptions, such as thinking like this: "If you don't want that promotion, you have a fixed mindset" or "If you don't want to grow your business, you have a fixed mindset." Not only is this not true, but this thinking itself might demonstrate a fixed mindset from the messenger.

Having a growth mindset is about beliefs we carry about ourselves and the world. It's a fundamental belief that our abilities are not set in stone; we can learn and adapt to multiple situations. People with a growth mindset see challenges as opportunities for growth, so they embrace new experiences, learn from failures, and focus on continuously improving themselves. Throughout the expat journey, we go through large amounts of change. Embracing a growth mindset enables you to perceive a moment of personal chaos as an opportunity to learn and grow rather than a barrier preventing you from thriving.

Another typical misconception about growth mindset is the tendency for individuals who previously embodied a growth mindset to adopt a fixed mindset once they reach major milestones (for example, a big promotion). The notion of "I made it to the top, now I know it all" reflects this fallacy, where their efforts to reach big goals become complacency.

As expats, we have the advantage of being exposed to various cultures and ways of thinking, so when making decisions, we can have a broader perspective and deeper understanding of the complexities involved. Over time, it's crucial to remain open-minded no matter how much knowledge you believe you have previously acquired. By seeking out new learnings, you can enhance your problem-solving skills, empathy, and adaptability.

Now that I have shared my points of view on growth mindset, let's go back to my story. You will see that life is full of moments oscillating between fixed and growth mindset.

2

THE MIDDLE CHILD SYNDROME?

It takes a lot of strength to take on the responsibility of looking within and causing your own human revolution.

-Larissa Rinaldi

If you google "middle child syndrome," you will find a lot of health and wellbeing websites attempting to define what this means. While this term has many definitions, the American Psychology Association (APA) hasn't recognized it as a legitimate syndrome and claims it is just a hypothetical condition.

While this is not a scientific term and mainly a popular belief, I cannot deny how I see myself as the typical middle child whose tendencies of diplomacy were developed early on.

My sister is two years older than me, and I am five years older than my brother. When we were growing up, my sister was "The Leader." And I, of course, was the follower who didn't question any of her decisions. She was articulate and had strong opinions, and I wanted to be able to do everything she did. My brother, on the other hand, was much more intelligent than us. He didn't just blindly follow her directions. And that's how the fights began.

Every time we fought, it was either my sister and I against him or my brother and I against my sister. Even though I was not always "The Peacemaker," there is something interesting to note here: it was never my brother and my sister against me.

They say the middle child tends to score higher on Agreeableness on the Big Five Personality Test[3]. Not only is that true for me, but I have also experienced this other

---

[3] Big Five is a framework that describes personalities in five groups: Openness to Experience, Conscientiousness, Extraversion, Agreeableness, and Neuroticism.

times in my life, and not just in my relationship with my siblings.

When I was in high school, my friend Galina[4] and I decided to start our own business: jewelry design. Galina and I would each share 50% of the business, and we agreed to spend a total of $100 on the wholesale stores at *Rua 25 de Março*[5] to buy supplies for our first pieces. I called my dad and asked him for $50 to start my business. He said, "Oh, do you want me to be your VC?" I didn't know what that meant, but I am sure he knew this was a high-risk investment, and I would likely lose everything. Although he questioned why I only needed $50, "Are you sure only $50 is enough?" he was probably certain we wouldn't see the profits of his investment.

So off we went to *Rua 25 de Março*. We purchased a lot of different supplies to create our trinket earrings. These earring styles were trendy in the late 90's in Brazil, so we were pretty confident of our imminent success. We built the first pieces, and considering we didn't have a lot of buyers in our tiny high school, Galina suggested we put them up for sale at her aunt's store. There was only one condition: we had to be at the store after school because her aunt only lent us the space; she wouldn't sell them for us.

I agreed to be there once or twice a week, as I had other commitments after school. Galina would do her shift on the other days. We sold a few things, but after a month or so, I noticed I was putting in more effort than my business

---

[4] Name changed to preserve individual's identity.
[5] Rua 25 de Março, or March 25th Street, is a major shopping district in São Paulo's historic center.

partner. I didn't really like her designs, and she was not very good with numbers. So, I quickly realized I became the main designer and finance manager of our business. And with the school finals approaching, I knew I had to dedicate more time to study than spending afternoons at her aunt's store (we didn't even have cell phones with Instagram and TikTok in the days of yore).

One day, during a school break, we sat on the staircase leading to the cafeteria for "the talk." I approached the conversation carefully, mindful of our friendship, but explained that our business wasn't working for me. To my surprise, she immediately agreed. We then discussed how to divide the remaining pieces and our sales revenue. This was the first difficult conversation I ever had in a business setting.

Maybe I didn't choose HR after all. Maybe HR chose me.

After graduating in Psychology and spending one year in the US, it was time to return home and start my career for good. My previous boss hired me to replace her in an HR Management role at a resort outside of São Paulo. She had gotten a well-deserved promotion at the corporate office, and I would lead the HR department for that resort with hundreds of employees and reporting directly to the General Manager.

It was really scary to be in charge. At only 25 years old, I was managing people and managing the entire HR function: budgets, goal setting, performance management, terminations. There were so many new things! I am sure I made many mistakes, especially in managing people. I had an assistant who, let's say, didn't have the best education and was falling behind because she didn't understand basic concepts. I failed her. I failed to use all those skills I've been developing since that first difficult conversation with my "business partner" in high school. I didn't know how to give her feedback.

As a young and new manager, I had the misguided belief that if I just told my subordinate what to do, things would get done exactly how I expected. At that time, I failed to have the courage or skills to have an open and honest conversation with this person. I didn't know exactly why she was not performing, nor did I take the time to understand it. I was frustrated. She was frustrated. And the work didn't progress the way I expected.

Additionally, I didn't have a great leader either at that workplace. My boss used to yell at people at all times, to the point that even those elegant 5-star resort guests could hear her screaming. Though she didn't yell at me directly, she used to say proudly that I was impartial. I learned in Psychology to have a poker face when dealing with clients, and I used that skill in dealing with her. But in retrospect, I shouldn't have been impartial. The environment was toxic. I can't count how many times people came to my office crying because she yelled at them. This was always a topic in exit interviews, too.

Over the years, I have had good bosses and bad bosses, and that will always be the case for all of us working in the corporate world. There is no competition for bad bosses, but I certainly know which one would take first place. During the financial crisis of 2008-2009, I decided to move back to São Paulo after living in Brasilia for a couple of years but was too afraid of being unemployed. So, I accepted the first offer I got.

The first red flag happened on my second day in this new job. They were absolutely super strict with arrival times. Everyone needed to be there by 9 am. It might seem reasonable to expect people to be in the office by 9 am, but in a city like São Paulo, with millions of people commuting every day (and all of them going to the Financial District), I had to give myself about two hours in the morning to arrive in the office on time.

So, on my second day, even though I was in the office neighborhood early enough, finding a parking lot with available space took me nearly half an hour. So finally, after parking my car, I arrived at the office at 9:04. I said good morning to my boss, who looked at the clock and went back to his computer screen without acknowledging me. So, I started leaving the house earlier. Around 8:30 am, I would have already parked the car and stopped at the nicest Starbucks I've ever been to for my morning cappuccino.

Several weeks later, this random man started talking to me as I was enjoying my coffee. When he asked where I was commuting from, which was my mom's house on the other side of the city, he was like, "Are you crazy? Why are you doing this? I bet you this job is not worth it. You need to leave the country, go study abroad or something." He went on and on about how commuting like this was unhealthy. I knew that already. He didn't need to remind me that what I really wanted to do was to leave the country.

So, at 8:55 am, I walked to the office to arrive just before 9 am. I asked my boss to have a 1:1. I explained to him that this was not working for me, so I was going to resign and go study abroad for some time. I've never been this impulsive. But that random chat at Starbucks probably just pushed me to do something I really wanted for quite some time.

My boss didn't accept my resignation. He offered me a big salary increase. I explained to him I was not having this conversation to negotiate a higher pay, but he knew that by earning more, I could rent a place near the office in the nicest neighborhood in the city. After a lot of dialogue, I ended up accepting his offer. He asked me to promise him I would never quit. I asked him to promise me he would never fire me. We didn't respond to each other's questions and moved on with our workday.

He always pushed me to do overtime even when I had finished all my work for the day. Most people in the office had already left, and all the lights were off, except for the one in the small office we shared.

One day, I shared with him the draft for the employee survey I was developing. In a poor attempt to provide feedback, he told me to sit by his desk. So I moved and took a seat across from him. He said I was being too direct on my survey questions and needed to go around people more instead of asking exactly what I wanted to hear from them. "For example, if I want to ask you out on a date, I won't ask you directly. I will grab your hands," as he moved to grab my hands, "...and I will caress them," as he was caressing my hands. I quickly moved them, got up, and wrapped everything up very quickly to leave for the day.

On another occasion, he made a comment about my skirt (a knee-length suit skirt) with this look on his face that made me feel like I was naked in front of him. Needless to say, I never wore that outfit again. So, yes, #MeToo.

But the middle child in me was the nice, diplomatic person who was afraid of saying anything because I didn't want to be awkward with anyone. Being impartial, complacent, and just going with the flow is just the middle child syndrome talking; it's not in agreement with the hideous management practices I've experienced early on.

It took me years to discover that I can manage up, provide feedback in a respectful and constructive manner, and not fear losing my job. But I didn't do this alone. I also learned to identify the people who were supportive and open to dialogue. That was the key to facilitating productive discussions.

3

HOW HR FOUND ME

*Humility is a superpower
that prevents overconfidence.*

-Morgan Housel

Very early on, when I was still in middle school, I became very curious about why people behave the way they do. Maybe it was the self-observation of my interactions with my siblings or watching my parents' marriage deteriorating in front of our eyes that sparked that curiosity. And there was an afternoon TV show with a Brazilian journalist named Sylvia Poppovic, who discussed human behavior with her guests, and many of them were psychologists. That's when I first started thinking about being a Psychologist "when I grow up."

During my high school years, I explored many professions, mostly in the fields of life sciences. I had a Biology teacher in high school who was really good at making us scared of his classes. On my first day there, I was new to that school, and slightly nervous if I would succeed, having spent the last few years in the public school system. That first day, my mom attended the Parents & Teachers conference, and this teacher did a good job scaring the parents as well. When we got home, my mom warned me that he seemed very strict and a lot of kids had failed his classes previously.

On the first day, he asked us to raise our hands if we wanted to go to college. Not surprisingly, all of us raised our hands. He then said with a firm tone, "ok, I will prepare you for *vestibular*."

My reaction was a mix of "I'm screwed" with "I wish all teachers were like him." After the first test, my grade was 4.5 out of 10. I thought that was bad, but it was one of the highest scores in the class. Still, I was nervous to tell my mom I got a *red* grade[6]. So, during dinner time, when she asked me about it, I told her it was 4.5, and in a sigh of relief, she said, "Wow, that's not too bad." I was like, "Wait. What? Who are you, and what you did to my mom?" Even my mom, who always expected high scores, knew this first test would be awful. So, after that, I spent hours nearly every day studying for his random tests and assignments. So, from the fear of failing in his discipline, I started to enjoy learning everything about cytology, histology, genetics, and ecosystems. I never got a 10 on his tests, but he was indeed the teacher who prepared me the most for any *vestibular*. I am grateful for that. Because of him, I nailed every Biology test on every college admission test. However, as we now know by now, it was not enough to secure a spot at a top public university.

My dad had a major financial loss during my first year in a private University. It was disconcerting to receive that news, and I spent the rest of the afternoon crying and picturing catastrophic scenes in my head about what the future could look like. The "catastrophic" image in my head was giving up my seat in this University that I was loving every moment and going to a cheaper and less prestigious school in the evening while working a full-time job during the day. I really didn't want that scenario to play out in the real world.

That day, I made the decision always to be financially independent and have a successful career.

---

[6] red grades are below passing grade and blue grades are above it – passing grade was a 7

I don't cry pretty. The next day, I likely woke up with puffy eyes and a red nose, still crying some tears, but I decided to go to school and talk to the Dean. It turns out he was a very approachable person and listened attentively to my story. He had this balanced approach of being empathetic and practical. After listening to my ill-fated story, he calmly told me that this was actually good timing as the University was launching a new scholarship program. He then advised me to write a letter to the scholarship department and "drop a few tears" in the letter. I did it. I filled out all the required forms, and a few weeks later, I had the response I wanted: I got a 100% scholarship. I was relieved but one of the conditions of the program was to be in good academic standing, so I was always afraid of failing any discipline. I was doing well. Even though I had never failed in school before, this time, I felt an extra pressure to succeed.

While juggling all the disciplines and mandatory internships, I was still searching for a paid internship. It was difficult to find a part-time position, as school demanded most of my free time. A couple of years later, my friend was doing an HR internship at a small boutique hotel in the heart of São Paulo. As she was wrapping up her internship, she said I should apply for her backfill position and told me I would be really good in HR because I was "organized."

Well, there you have it. I got into HR because I was organized.

I remember how anxious I was on my first day. I had no idea what it meant to go to the same place every day to do "work," whatever that entailed. I recall we had spreadsheets to record employee training. There were small, color-coded squares in an Excel file representing the type of training and number of hours of training. I was so afraid to mess up with that spreadsheet. But I didn't. I had a very supportive manager who let me experiment and try new things. The hotel had a quality certification, and I soon became an internal ISO 9001 auditor. When HR was being audited, I inserted myself and confidently responded to their questions. We always had great scores during those audits, and I am proud to have contributed to our results (and grateful for the trust my manager had in me!).

Part of the ISO 9001 requirement was a minimum of hours of employee training. We didn't have a budget to bring external consultants (a blessing in disguise), and after watching my manager create lots of training programs, I had the courage to ask if I could do one by myself. The first workshop I developed was "Effective Communications," which included how to communicate properly, how to give feedback, how to avoid gossip (a very important topic for hotel employees!). I brought some of the knowledge I was learning in school to group dynamics and created a number of activities during the session to support their learning. I nailed that session. I receive a lot of compliments. I felt good. And I knew then I wanted to get more into employee development.

In the meantime, I still had all my obligations with the University and it was time to select three areas for the mandatory internships in our last year of school. That's the year we started seeing "real patients." At that point, I had already been doing my HR internship for one year and could use that as an internship in Organizational Psychology. But I was still interested in exploring other areas, and as if my day had 30 hours, I decided to stretch myself and pick 3 other elective disciplines: Clinical Psychology (where my patient was a young woman having issues with her family dynamics), Community Psychology (which was an internship at an outpatient Psychiatric hospital), and Hospital Psychology (at a public women's hospital).

I had been waiting for five years to finally intern at a hospital. Don't ask me why because I wouldn't know how to answer, but I always loved hospitals. I loved the smell of hospitals, and I thought I wanted to work at one. So, I was assigned to this large women's public hospital in São Paulo, that mostly treats female cancer (breast, ovaries, etc.).

Initially, I had this supervisor who was very sweet. She was an Italian woman who always greeted me with *"Ciao, Bella!"* but she was also very pregnant and soon went on maternity leave. My new supervisor was a middle-aged man who had this "all-business" look on his face. He didn't greet me *"Ciao, Bella"* but he made me read all the medical literature related to breast cancer. He always told me that as psychologists, if we want to be respected by the doctors, we need to know what they know, read what they read, and speak their language. Every week, he gave me a lot of articles to read and then quizzed me. I guess I learned how to apply this mindset when I transitioned to an HR leadership position later in my career. But I didn't know what to do with my career yet. I was still wondering if I would ever apply for a full-time job at a hospital.

Every week, I saw a handful of patients in the chemotherapy room. I would approach one at a time and start talking with them. Sometimes, I would start with what they knew about their disease, how they received their diagnosis, and what their expectations were. I was shocked that many of these women came from rural areas very distant from São Paulo and barely had any knowledge about cancer. So, many times, they received a late diagnosis, when the cancer was already advanced.

Hearing all those stories, I wondered how I could possibly help them. Every time, I had this feeling of "I have no idea what I am doing here." The most difficult time was when a young woman, probably in her 20's, approached me because her mom was dying. My naïve-self thought she wanted to discuss how to say goodbye and how deeply she would miss her mother. I was wrong. She was angry. She started saying how awful her mom was. She didn't care her mom was dying but others thought she should react differently, and this was her struggle. She just wanted the world to know she hated her dying mother and probably wanted people to stop expecting any other reaction from her. I have no recollection of how I dealt with that probably because it was painful for me to even try to help this woman.

Every time after my hospital visits, I had this feeling of being better as an HR practitioner than as a hospital psychologist. By the end of the school year, which was also my graduation, I was glad to have experienced that, so I had more clarity now about what I didn't want to do. I wanted to work as far as possible from hospitals. I couldn't feel the excitement in the hospital smell anymore.

Now, a little over twenty years after my graduation and a collection of roller coaster rides on my career journey, most around me consider me a successful person.

There are key moments in our lives when we must make big decisions: what would be my major, what career path will I follow, and should I leave everything behind and relocate across the ocean?

When I look back, there were so many times I saw myself at a crossroads. The decisions I made at each point took me where I am today. When I was offered the job in San Francisco, I was also offered the option to go to Seattle instead. But I wouldn't even get any of these offers if I was happy in my previous job (i.e. if I worked for a boss that didn't sexually harass his female employees). But the only reason I went to work for that creepy boss, to begin with, was because, before that, I was living in Brasilia. This city quickly became my favorite city in Brazil, but it was a place centered around the government. It would be more difficult to have a successful career in the private sector there, so then I decided to move back to São Paulo. I could go on and on, dissecting each big decision I made in my life, and I always wonder where I would be now if I had taken another turn at one of those intersections.

These are just some of life's conundrums, and I think that what helped me find my path was my ability to stay curious and accept that neither decision was right nor wrong; they were just different.

There is a moment when we come to terms with the fact that perfection and imperfection exist on a spectrum. In this expat journey, when we start working with so many people outside of our bubble who are different from us, we might have a natural instinct to protect our ego and be defensive about those nuances in communication styles, ways of thinking, and living. When you start opening up to these new cultures, it may make you feel disconnected or not yourself anymore, but it's just an early sign that you are learning and growing.

Nowadays, when I am coaching individuals or teams, I like to use the Mood Elevator framework, developed by Sean Lenn[7] (2017), which offers a useful exercise to reframe your experiences and reset your curious spirit. It charts our moods in a continuum, from the lowest levels of sadness, anger, and judgment to the peaks of appreciation, resourcefulness, and gratitude. We all encounter daily situations that might push us toward the bottom of the mood elevator. Generally, people associate how they feel with external events: you didn't get the consulate appointment the day you wanted, flight prices increased, your boss didn't recognize your contribution to a project, and the list goes on. All of these events stimulate your thoughts ("I should have purchased that flight last week!") and those thoughts drive your emotions. So, you might feel irritated, anxious, or angry.

---

[7] Senn, L. (2017). The Mood Elevator. Berrett-Koehler Publishers.

Figure 1
The Mood Elevator (Senn, 2017)

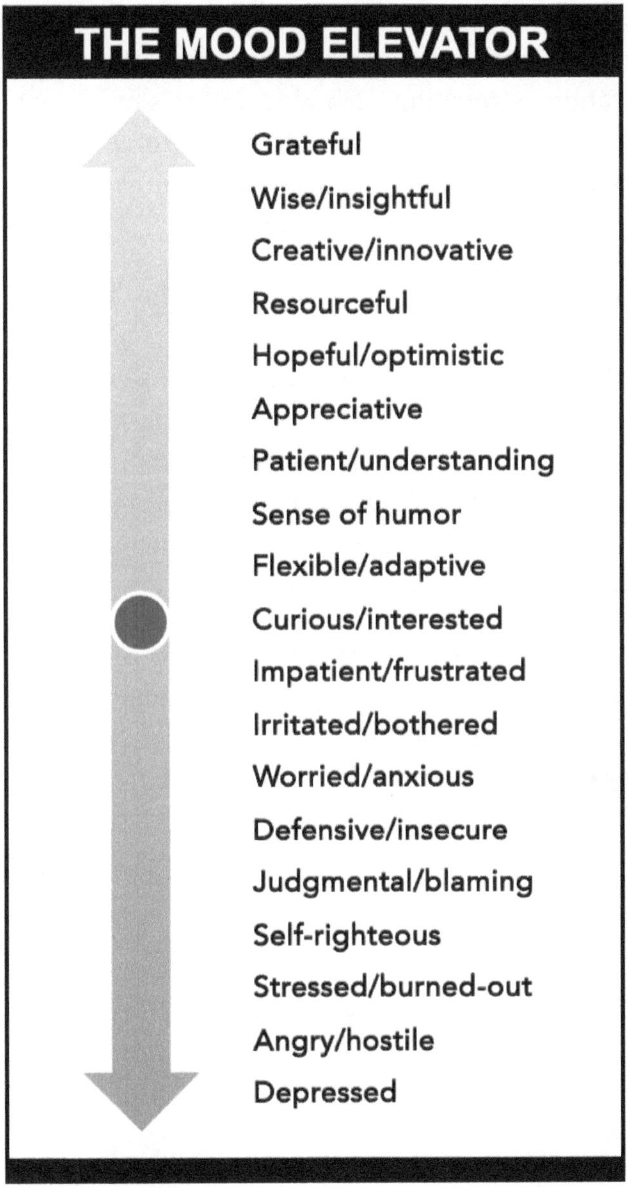

THE MOOD ELEVATOR

↑
- Grateful
- Wise/insightful
- Creative/innovative
- Resourceful
- Hopeful/optimistic
- Appreciative
- Patient/understanding
- Sense of humor
- Flexible/adaptive
- Curious/interested
- Impatient/frustrated
- Irritated/bothered
- Worried/anxious
- Defensive/insecure
- Judgmental/blaming
- Self-righteous
- Stressed/burned-out
- Angry/hostile
- Depressed

↓

When you are already feeling at the bottom of the mood elevator, some grounding techniques borrowed from Cognitive Behavioral Therapy will help you reconnect to the present moment and alleviate some of those negative feelings. Some techniques include breathing exercises, meditation, stretching, drinking water slowly, reading a poem or inspirational quote, listening to relaxing music, and many others. Find the one that inspires you and try it next time you feel negative emotions.

But the key to avoiding reaching the bottom of the elevator is to stay curious. In the book *Why?*[8] Mario Livio (2017) explores human curiosity and teaches us that "curiosity may be a powerful source of motivation for its own sake" (p. 79), that means, gaining additional information is in itself rewarding for our brains and might help alleviate the anxiety of all the unknowns we face when we are moving to a whole new place.

So next time you notice yourself feeling lower-level sentiments or you find yourself at a crossroads, ask yourself curious questions: what word describes what you are feeling? What makes you feel this way? What steps can you take today to improve yourself?

---

[8] Livio, M. (2017). *Why?: what makes us curious.* Simon & Schuster.

4

THE BLOGGER

―∞―

Fight for the things you care about. But do it in a way that will lead others to join you.

-Ruth Bader Ginsburg

During my last year in university, my friend said she was planning a trip to the Amazon and wanted to talk to someone at the on-campus travel agency during our break. I went with her, and while she was discussing her trip with a travel agent, I was browsing some brochures. One of them was about a program called "Au Pair in America." When I touched that brochure, the travel agent shifted her conversation to me and made a comment about how affordable it was for a one-year interexchange program. I was immediately interested. I needed about one thousand US dollars to live abroad for one year with a host family and study whatever I wanted.

Later, I went to the hotel where I was still doing my HR internship and mentioned this program to my manager. She gave me the support and courage to go forward.

The next step would be to tell my mom. When she picked me up that evening, I got into the car and laughingly said, "I will live in the US for a year." She initially demonstrated a mix of curiosity and cynicism and responded, "How?" and I told her about the program. It seemed safe and affordable and would be the perfect opportunity to improve my English skills. The timing was perfect, too, because the application and placement process took approximately 6 to 8 months, and that was the exact amount of time I had until graduation.

My mom was always very connected to the family. She refused to move to a different neighborhood in São Paulo – which would have made her commute way easier – just so she could stay near my grandma. This is to paint the picture for you, dear reader, so you can understand how surprised I was when she responded, "Yes, you should go."

From that moment, that was my approach; instead of telling people, "I am thinking about this," I started telling my family and close friends, "I am going" in a very assertive manner, almost like I was putting out to the universe that this is happening and cannot go wrong.

This was the year 2003 when life existed without social media. So, I started searching the internet for more information about the program, found blogs of current and prospective Au Pairs, and started reading their open diaries.

That inspired me to create my own blog, which still lives in the historical archives of the internet. In the blog era, the way we "friended" people by linking their blogs to ours. So that's how I connected with other Au Pairs who are still great friends of mine.

As I started blogging more, I learned basic HTML to be able to change the design of my blog, add different fonts and colors, and add pictures and gadgets. And, of course, a section on the side of the page with links to my favorite Au Pair blogs.

As I detailed on my blog, the day-to-day experience with the kids, family, school, and my new friends, eventually, many other Au Pairs were also following me. The day after my birthday, I made a post describing my day and showed pictures of my gifts, including this beautiful Kate Spade pink shoulder bag that my host family gave to me. Months later, when I met a new Au Pair in person, welcoming her to our cluster, she recognized me: "You're Pati-Au-Pair, right? I love that Kate Spade bag you got for your birthday." So, yes, I was kind of an influencer before influencers were invented.

I was a very successful Au Pair. Not just because I was very lucky to be matched with the best family I could, but from early on, I was focused on enjoying my three hundred and sixty-five days abroad. I knew when the program was going to end, so I wanted to enjoy every single moment of this big sabbatical.

The first encounter with my host family was, as expected, a mix of excitement and awkwardness. Host mom and the kids went to the hotel in Stamford, CT, where orientation had taken place during that first week, to pick me up. It was about a 30-40-minute ride from the hotel to my new home. Host mom worked from home, whereas host dad was an executive for a large firm in New York City during weekdays and came home on the weekend. I knew very well what the host family and the Au Pair's obligations were in the program, and I was soon happily surprised by their generosity, sense of humor, support, and overall perspective in life. They became like a real family to me.

My kids were school age (boy 7-8, girl 10-11), so they were pretty independent, and my duties consisted of waking up at 6:30 am (this was actually the most difficult part of the day), wake the kids up, prepare their lunch, make sure they get on the school bus. At 3 pm, I had to be home when the kids got back from school and then help to prepare dinner. Once or twice a week, I also had to do the kids' laundry.

During the day, while the kids were at school, I frequently hung out with my Au Pair friends. I always took the time to greet new Au Pairs, picked them up, drove around town to show them the places I liked, and offered support as they were adapting to their new lives.

One of my best memories with my host family was my skiing experience. During winter break, we spent one week in Stowe, VT. The kids were enrolled in ski school during the day. My host family offered to pay for a class for me on my first day. I was super excited to try this new sport, but I guess none of them had much confidence that I would enjoy it because "none of the previous Brazilian Au Pairs did well skiing." Sorry for them; they are missing out! On the first day, I went to my morning level 1 downhill skiing group class. After class, I would meet up with my host family at the lodge. When the class ended, the instructor said that I did very well and could skip to level 3 on the following day if I wanted to. I went back to the lodge, anxious to tell my family how well this Brazilian did.

There was a minor hiccup, though. I had learned to put my skis on and learned the basics of pizza skiing, but when I got to the front of the lodge, I didn't even know how to remove the skis. I found an instructor who had a look on his face, "How did you get here?" but he taught me how to remove my skis; we laughed a little bit about it and went on with our days.

The rest of my day was even better. Host dad took me and the kids on some runs, and when we were going up the lift, he realized he had gotten the wrong lift that would take us to a slightly more difficult run. And then I learned another life lesson: when you are on the top of the hill, you just have to let go of any self-judgment and do the best you can. *There is only one way I am going down this hill: I will ski.* I didn't want to feel like a loser who gives up (not that I believe nowadays that giving up is for losers, but that's how I felt at that moment), so I just paid attention to what others were doing, learned a few new skills, and kept following my host family through those runs all week long. By the end of the week, I was following them on a black diamond trail.

I felt so good skiing. For the first time in my life, I was good at a sport. I was always the one who made up excuses in school to skip Physical Education classes (because they always involved playing one of these sports: volleyball, handball, or basketball. I hated playing each one of them), so doing something that I knew I could become good at was a major confidence booster. Hearing my host family and their friends praising me also felt amazing, of course. Nearly twenty years later, when I saw the family's friends at a wedding, one of them immediately said, "Look who's here: the skier!" Yes, I am a legend in the beginner category.

But during that Au Pair year, not everyone was as lucky as I was with their host family matching, and not everyone adapted as well, even if they had good host families. But my advice to them was always to enjoy their experience as much as possible because we knew there was an expiration date. This was just a big adventure for us to improve ourselves, and in the worst-case scenario, if this didn't work out, we could go back to our home country and be with our loved ones. If the "worst-case" scenario is good, the rest cannot be bad, right? (This was my thinking process in my early 20's. I am still a very optimistic person, but I understand not everyone has the privilege of having supportive families to go back to.)

The lesson learned for me at that moment is that we always have choices, and even though there is always a luck factor in everything we do in life, we are not 100% victims of fate. We just need to be aware of what we are leaving behind when we are making life choices and anticipate the bumps in the road as much as possible. But, sometimes, the hardest part is to leave behind parts of ourselves.

And that's when I had the cultural shock. After twelve months of living the dream in a small town in Connecticut, I was back in the chaos of São Paulo. I was a grown-up, looking for a job, no longer driving an Audi or having long lunches with my friends every day. Real life welcomed me back with arms wide open. Soon after, I got my first full-time job, and the hustle began.

5

BEING AUTHENTIC

―∞―

There is no way out of the imagined order. When we break down our prison walls and run towards freedom, we are in fact running into the more spacious exercise yard of a bigger prison.

-Yuval Noah Harrari

I typically define São Paulo's corporate life as very traditional and hierarchical. During the first several years of my career, I led the Human Resources departments of multiple hotels and resorts. My days were filled with processes, controls, rules, do's and don'ts. I wore a black suit every day (not by choice) with a white top and black leather shoes, had my hair done in a sleek low ponytail, wore small and delicate jewelry, had my nails done every week with a transparent or light beige nail polish, and the final touch was natural-looking make-up.

As much as I understood the need to look professional, I never understood why I had to follow the same rules as customer-facing employees since I spent most of my day inside an office space. I was a young professional in my 20s and wanted to wear different colors and different nail polishes whenever I felt like it (and still look professional!). But I once heard a male manager saying that women who work in hospitality cannot wear red nail polish because guests would confuse them with prostitutes. [Eye roll]. As much as I disliked these rules, they were a part of the world I lived in, and I simply complied with them.

Obviously, the work environment is much more than what we wear or what time we are required to arrive at work, but it tells a lot about the company's culture. Frederic Laloux[9], a renowned coach, facilitator, and author, describes this type of company as the Conformist organization. In those cultures, organizations "operate on the hidden assumption that there is one way of doing

---

[9] Laloux, F. (2014). Reinventing organizations: A guide to creating organizations inspired by the next stage in human consciousness. Las Vegas: Nelson Parker

things," they have replicable processes, strict rules, clear structures, and hierarchies. Too much initiative is not well seen, and instruction and guidance must come from the top.

After years working for industries and managers who were so strict with their rules, I decided that I couldn't do that anymore. Feeling so restricted in what seemed to me a too rigid environment, I started questioning my professional choices and wondered if I should even try a career outside of Human Resources. However, soon after, I discovered that I could do a similar type of work in a different culture. And that's how I found the passion for HR again.

At that stage in my career, I had just joined a US-based tech start-up. The work itself was not much different from the work I had been doing in the previous years. Although I was the solo HR practitioner in Brazil for this company, my boss was in London, and the headquarters was in San Francisco. My world instantly expanded. I felt I could learn from others and have my voice heard. I finally could be myself at work. Small things like not having a dress code or a specific arrival time made such a big difference. I was still dressing up to work and being one of the first to arrive in the office every morning, but that was my choice, not because there was a made-up rule that we all had to follow without questioning. I felt my authentic self.

A few years later, I was offered a position in San Francisco. During those initial years living abroad, my sense of being authentic was a little shaken again. This time, it was for a different reason. Most expats probably feel that it is very different to speak "fluently" a second language and use it on your vacation, social interactions, or sporadic business meetings. Well, you guessed it. Thinking and speaking in a second language in a business setting all day long was much more challenging.

Having my brain operating at its max throughout my workday, trying to make sense of everything happening around me, and speaking in my second language was brutal in those initial weeks and months. By the end of my workday, I would arrive home with a headache, take a nap, cook dinner, watch some TV, and decompress a little to start all over the next day.

As I was building my life in a new country, I started feeling like I had "two personalities." I felt like I was one person when I was in Brazil speaking Portuguese and felt like another person in the US speaking English. The former is a confident professional and the joker of the family. The latter is vulnerable and struggles even to crack a knock-knock joke.

It took years for me to feel comfortable and accept that I would never again feel 100% Brazilian or 100% anything else. But I also don't need to absolutely reject my Brazilian self to feel part of American society. Nowadays, I am the first one to make jokes about my own accent or call myself "bye-lingual" when I forget words in both languages (and this keeps happening more often).

I am fortunate that my current employer has offices in Brazil and Portugal, so I get to experience my native language in a professional setting again. Being part of a company that not only respects my diverse background but actually recognizes the value I bring for speaking Portuguese fluently and having a deep cultural understanding of the regions they operate has helped integrate those "two personalities" that I've felt divided between for many years.

That feeling of being an authentic leader goes far beyond how I express myself or whichever language I am speaking. I learned HR in a generation that people would typically say, "You leave your personal life out of the door when you go to work." I never believed that. Whatever is happening in our personal lives shows up at work. So, I think it's better to embrace it and acknowledge to ourselves what we are feeling in that moment so we can actually move on and focus on the work in front of us.

As I consistently continue to develop myself, I now see I can influence people to see others as the whole person, not just that rigid professional following processes and complying with rules. Yet, I consistently catch myself wondering, "Am I being professional enough here?" "What would people think about this?" "What if I rub someone the wrong way?" In the end, all I want is for me to be accepted for who I am and create a space for others to express themselves in their most authentic way.

6

LIFE IN THE SILICON VALLEY

Only the man who builds the future has a right to judge the past.

-Nietzsche

"We don't want to be profitable; our focus is on growth." That was the answer from a start-up CEO in San Francisco when I asked him if his start-up was profitable yet. His answer was jaw-dropping for me at that time. And based on the look on his face, he probably thought my question was pretty dumb. I was still new to San Francisco and its highly entrepreneurial environment. This idea went against everything I learned in business school. What do you mean you don't want to be profitable? I couldn't get my head around that.

I grew up in São Paulo in the 1980s. Back then, Brazil was going through an era of hyperinflation. Prices increased almost daily, and currency typically changed too. Because of inflation, an item that would cost one million of whatever currency there was would become a thousand, as the government had a practice of slashing the three last zeros and changing the name of the currency more frequently than I could keep up with.

My mom used to give me money every day to buy food and snacks in the school cafeteria. I used to buy the same sandwich every day (my favorite then was a *Bauru*: grilled ham and cheese with tomatoes[10]). During break, I would go to the cafeteria, place my order, and ask the same question every day: "How much is it today?"

Early on, my dad taught us the importance of saving money. We received part of our monthly allowance in cash, and the other part would go to a savings account called

---

[10] This is the simplified version of a Bauru. The original Bauru includes mayo and replaces the ham for roast beef and is considered since 2018 an Intangible Cultural Heritage of the State of São Paulo

"overnight," a type of investment in which interest accrued overnight. This was a decent investment because inflation was so high, and the economy was all over. Then, in 1990, Brazil elected its first democratic president after over two decades of military dictatorship. This "genius" president blocked all savings accounts, allowing for a very small limit. That money disappeared. I was frustrated; all the money from our allowance that we were saving to buy a new fancy vinyl music player had vanished *overnight*.

Later, in 1994, we had a new president who implemented a series of changes to stabilize the economy. Over the years, and especially after I entered the workforce, I started paying attention to another issue: high-interest rates. I learned quickly that you should never, ever, have credit card debt.

Given all this context, you can probably imagine my shock when I learned people in the US had credit card debt and start-ups didn't care about profits (this is obviously a very generalized statement but describes what I felt early on).

Growing up in troubled economic times in Brazil definitely shaped me to have a different relationship with money. But once I started embedding myself in the Silicon Valley culture, I started seeing things from a new perspective.

The work environment in corporate São Paulo, as I described in another chapter, is much more formal and hierarchical. Silicon Valley, on the other hand, is probably the most innovative market in the world.

To bring that level of innovation, minds and organizations cannot operate with the same systems and beliefs as other corporate cultures. The workforce is so diverse in the Bay Area that we are faced with different perspectives at all times.

I've seen many times companies in other places trying to incorporate start-up values into their businesses. But the problem with this is that a lot of times, people think that to operate like a start-up you just need to get rid of your formal dress code and put a ping-pong table in the break room to engage people. You might get people excited in the beginning, but it won't add any value nor will hold the initial excitement in the long run.

After joining a tech start-up and moving to the Bay Area, the contrast became clear. In this culture, people can have more autonomy, which fundamentally carries a level of responsibility that people from a very hierarchical culture have never experienced before.

One of the key philosophies of Silicon Valley is to fail fast. It is challenging to evolve our thinking when we have always been surrounded by people who conform to the rules so they can earn or keep their status in a group, such as the corporate life in São Paulo where I learned HR. Even though I didn't feel comfortable with that type of environment, that's how I learned to work. You create processes, you follow processes, and you don't question them [much]. Rinse and repeat. If you are a good process follower, you have a higher status in the organization.

Once I started to understand that there are ways to systematically learn from mistakes and iterate, I started feeling less vulnerable and more confident to question my and others' thinking and ways of working.

Despite the expression "work smarter, not harder" being a cliché, it resonates with me when I compare corporate São Paulo of twenty years ago (the time when I entered the workforce) to what I experience in the Bay Area. Frankly, my opinion might be biased based on my own career development. But I have a sense that in São Paulo, I was always busy with something, worked long hours, and most of the time focused on tasks that "must get done," but a lot of times didn't add value to the business. We were busy for the sake of being busy. In the world of Silicon Valley, even when start-ups that cannot make a lot of investments in fancy software to automate every single HR task so that we, HR practitioners, can focus on more strategic work, I feel that the work style is more evolved than what I experienced down in the South Hemisphere.

But it's a little of a bubble, too. One time, I met with a vendor that had developed a mobile app for performance management. Because everyone says that "everything needs to be mobile," this individual thought it would be a good idea to have a mobile-only performance review process. Now think with me. We sit in front of a computer all day long to perform most, if not all, of the work. Why do I need to turn to another device to complete my team's performance assessment? I clearly remember how many times they proudly emphasized in the meeting that this HR system was mobile-only (I'm glad I didn't take a shot every time they said "mobile-only"). This was just one of the "features" of this system, and everything else they showed, unfortunately, was a flop. I couldn't wait for them to leave because they had no idea how to do performance management, but they had an idea and resources. I hope they ~~failed~~ learned. Fast.

While I was pretty impatient in that meeting, I understand that this type of interaction needs to happen for innovation to take place. No one is successful with one grand idea the first time they try. And if they are, I'm sure luck played a big role, not solely competence.

The pace of change in the work environment has been faster than ever, especially after the pandemic. There is no going "back to normal." I guess the concept of normal has changed, too. Drawing from the world of software development, Jeffrey Hull[11] offers a fresh perspective on leadership development. Just like in software, where the Beta product is unfinished and still has bugs to be fixed, people are also a work in progress. The goal is not perfection, but it's about ongoing learning, evolving, and adapting ourselves to every new situation we are challenged with.

---

[11] Hull, J. (2019). Flex: The art and science of leadership in a changing world. New York: TarcherPerigee.

7

I SPEAK FUNNY

Above all, it is necessary for a person to have a true self-estimate.

-Seneca

I moved to San Francisco in my early 30's and single. I wanted to be social and make new friends. There were many aspects of communicating in a second language that became apparent right away.

First, I noticed people's tone of voice would change when they realized I had an accent and English was not my native language. In my head, all I could think was, "Dude, I just have an accent. I am not deaf." Situations like this were common but became just a source of laughter for my friends and me.

But as time went by, I started noticing some deeply rooted biases that can be hurtful when you are still feeling vulnerable and trying to do your best. After several months in my new job, it was time for the performance review. Never in my career have I felt threatened or afraid of a review, and always faced as an opportunity to learn more and develop myself.

A few minutes before the meeting with my boss, I received the written review online so we could discuss it during the meeting. For context, my first big project in this new role was the global implementation of a new recruiting system. I loved that project and was very proud to have been able to implement it in just a few months. In my written review, my boss seemed to agree with that sentiment and wrote a paragraph about my great performance in that project, adding that I executed it "flawlessly." That word stuck with me because first, I had to Google translate it (yes, Google Translate was my best friend for many years). And having my own boss think I performed so well in this very important project made me feel good and validated.

But as I continued reading her assessment, I was surprised when I saw that she marked the option "needs improvement" on the competency "communication." But she didn't add any comments. Just that. In my head, I was thinking, *Hello, management 101, you shouldn't provide criticism without explaining or giving examples.* But that was it. I had just a couple of minutes left before our in-person meeting.

During the meeting, everything was going well. She continued to emphasize my "flawless execution" on that project, and we were about to wrap up the meeting when she asked if I had any questions. In my head, I was thinking, *Oh, yes, I have so many questions,* and I politely asked her to provide more insights about her assessment of my communication skills. Based on her facial reaction, I don't think she was expecting me to actually ask any questions. But I was really curious. If I was able to "flawlessly" implement a system and train hundreds of people worldwide, what parts of my communication needed improvement? I am sure there was something, but she couldn't articulate it. She had an awkward look on her face and eventually said, "Hmm, well... is that... hmmm... you know... when you speak... hmmm... you have an accent." I was in shock she actually said that out loud. I was so new here. Obviously, I had an accent (spoiler alert, I still have an accent). This doesn't describe any issue if there is an issue. For years, I wanted to remove my accent completely. I knew it was a difficult task, but I was always questioning my own skills and capabilities because I had an accent.

I now know that my accent comes from my angst to get the ideas out of my head as quickly as possible. I am a proud *Paulista* (aka, someone from São Paulo, Brazil), and I am aware that I speak very fast in Portuguese. Many years ago, during an internship at a psychiatric day hospital, we did a series of Art Therapy sessions with some of the patients. One day, when describing an activity to a patient, aware that I spoke very fast and attempting to ensure the patient understood the task, I explained it very, very slowly. He interrupted me and said, "Doctor, I am crazy, not stupid." We both laughed, I apologized, and we moved on.

Speaking another language was always challenging because I couldn't speak at the same speed as I was used to. I realized that this was one of the areas that impacted my ability to communicate clearly.

After living in the US for a year or so, I was on a business trip with my boss and a couple of teammates. We rented a car, and I was the one looking at Google Maps on my phone and providing directions to my boss, who was behind the wheel. I wanted to be funny, so I started providing directions with that "robotic" voice similar to a GPS voice. My colleagues and my boss were astonished. They said, "When you speak like a GPS, you don't have an accent!" We laughed about this, and every now and then, I would use my GPS voice for their amusement.

But I cannot talk like a GPS all the time because, afterall, I am human. When we all speak, we speak with emotion and not just like we were reading directions from a manual. So yes, I continue to have an accent.

Many years later, when I had finished my coaching certification, a friend introduced me to an executive coach who was willing to share with me her own lessons learned about building a career as a coach. We had a good and engaging phone call, and, in the end, she added, "Well, there is one more thing. You know, I am from [country in Europe] but learned English in the UK, so I speak with a British accent..." – she did not sound British, by the way – "...and people in the US think British people sound smarter." I listened attentively, wondering where this story was going, and she completed, "You have an accent from a third-world country... executives have prejudice; they won't want to work with you." Who really has prejudice? Once again, I was dumbfounded someone had the nerve to assess my competence based on my accent. I thanked her for her perspective, and soon after, we finished the call.

Internally, I was still digesting what I heard. The first thought that came to mind was, *F*** you, bitch*, but I knew I had to decouple the discriminatory remarks from the actual feedback to learn something about this situation.

While I completely disagree that I am not as credible because I have an accent or executives won't want to work with me because of my Brazilian accent (have you been to the SF Bay Area? Everyone has an accent!), it always bothered me when I say something and the person says "Ahn?" or "you speak funny, what is that about?"

So, I decided to find a speech coach. I tried a couple of different coaches, but one was too expensive. I didn't like the approach of the other one, but then I finally found someone with a lot of experience with expats, and I immediately felt there was chemistry!

From the beginning, my speech coach told me my English was already really good. My accent was not very thick, but we would work together to improve my pronunciation, not remove my accent. I was a little disappointed hearing that – I wanted to remove my accent completely – but as the sessions progressed, and she continued to give me new exercises and provide feedback on my progress, I started feeling good about it. And I finally came to terms with the fact that I was not going to remove my accent. I will be who I am, and my accent is part of my story and my accomplishments. My commitment to myself is not to erase where I came from but to always become the best version of myself. So, I learned to slow down and articulate my phonemes more clearly. And, if you ask today where my accent is from, it's from knowledge and life experience. That's where it's from.

From that interaction with my patience in the psychiatric hospital and throughout my career, I learned how critical **self-awareness** is for any successful leader. Even more so, as expats we must have clarity about our own strengths, weaknesses, and cultural biases so we can successfully navigate in a new environment. For example, when a person says something or does something that provokes a reaction ("You have a third-world country accent"), understanding your own underlying triggers is crucial for addressing them appropriately.

Self-awareness is one of the components of **emotional intelligence**, according to Daniel Goleman's[12] model. Alongside self-awareness, his model emphasizes **self-regulation, motivation, empathy,** and **social skills** as critical pillars. The ability to recognize, understand, manage, and utilize our emotions effectively is key to being a successful leader. In fact, research shows that emotional intelligence is a strong predictor of career success[13].

No one can deny these skills are important to any person alive on this planet, but I would argue that they're even more critical when we move to a new country. We are social beings, and we can live a happier life when we immerse ourselves in the community and cultivate healthy relationships that can alleviate the feelings of loneliness and homesickness, as well as navigate the ups and downs of this big adventure called the expat life.

---

[12] Coleman, D & Bradberry, T. (2017, February 9). Emotional Intelligence Has 12 Elements. Which Do You Need to Work On? Harvard Business Review. https://hbr.org/2017/02/emotional-intelligence-has-12-elements-which-do-you-need-to-work-on

[13] Urquijo, I., Extremera, N., & Azanza, G. (2019). The Contribution of Emotional Intelligence to Career Success: Beyond Personality Traits. *International journal of environmental research and public health, 16*(23), 4809. https://doi.org/10.3390/ijerph16234809

8

SQUEEZING INTO A BOX

∞

Pigeonholing is something people need to do in order to feel that they have set the chaos of existence into some kind of reassuring order.

-Elizabeth Gilbert

Passport to Growth

Remember that one manager who thought my job performance was not as good because I had an accent? Yes, she did it again. A few months after I moved to San Francisco, she decided one day that we all needed to do a "spring cleaning" in our office. Indeed, that office was pretty messy and needed some TLC[14].

My colleagues and I started moving things around, getting rid of unnecessary documents and objects no longer needed, etc. In the middle of that chaos, our boss had some objects in her hand, looked at me and said: *"Basura!"* I was really confused. What does she mean? What is this? Those few seconds felt like an eternity. I didn't want to look dumb, but I had no idea what she was saying.

My colleague (not a coincidence, my best friend nowadays) intercepted the "dialogue" and said, "She speaks Portuguese, not Spanish." In a sigh of relief, I thought to myself, "Ahh, this is Spanish." Our boss then added, "Isn't it all the same?" Hmm, nope.

I grew up in São Paulo as an unknowingly privileged white middle-class girl. Growing up as a typical middle-class family, there were times we faced financial ups and downs, but we always overcame obstacles and never really struggled to make ends meet. So, I had a romanticized belief that when people work harder, they can be more successful.

---

[14] TLC stands for Tender Loving Care

When I moved to the US, I was no longer that white middle-class girl but an immigrant from Latin America, a Latina. That conflict with my own identity and being forced to see the world through these new lenses helped me better understand where I came from and realize the issues that other people have that I luckily didn't have.

That Saramago quote I shared in the introduction of this book, "You have to leave the island to see the island," always stood out to me because as I reflect on my own history, things started making much more sense once "I left the island." I immigrated to the USA over ten years ago, and as the years go by, not only am I able to better understand the American culture, but I am also able to see myself and my own culture from a different and maybe less biased point of view.

It might feel counter-intuitive, but I think I was only able to broaden my perspective because of all those assumptions people made about me, which many times were insulting and hurtful. People typically make assumptions about others depending on how we talk, how we dress, where we grew up, etc.

I was constantly asked (and sometimes still am) if Brazilians are Latin or not (spoiler alert: the US doesn't think so[15]), if schools in Brazil are good enough, how people can learn a second language there, if we speak Spanish

---

[15] Pew Research Center. (2023, April 19). How a coding error provided a rare glimpse into Latino identity among Brazilians in the U.S. Pew Research Center. https://www.pewresearch.org/short-reads/2023/04/19/how-a-coding-error-provided-a-rare-glimpse-into-latino-identity-among-brazilians-in-the-u-s/

(*basura!*), among other microaggressions hidden as curiosities.

A couple of months after I moved to San Francisco, a friend of mine set me up on a blind date with her friend. As we were talking about ourselves, where we came from, among other first-date types of subjects, I started to notice some implicit bias in the way he talked to me. At some point, he asked point blank in what year we got internet in Brazil. Right there, I knew what he was implying. And I was shocked.

I came from one of the largest cities in the world, and despite never being rich, I had access to technology earlier than most average Americans. The implicit assumption here is that I came from the poor, jungle, third-world country, therefore, I was an uneducated, uncultured, and needed-to-be-saved immigrant. Don't get me wrong. He was a very nice gentleman, but many people have this assumption amplified by Hollywood movies that America (and North-Americans) are the best of the world and need to save the rest of the poor us. And as nice as people are, those assumptions and microaggressions come out of their mouths without them realizing how they come across.

But back to the issue of "Are Brazilians Latinos or not?" I never liked to check any box, not because I deny the country where I was born is in the Latin America region, but because I always had a bias against being forced into one box.

Latin America is such a huge region with so much diversity in terms of culture, food, and history that I don't think it's fair nor do I feel celebrated putting us all in one small box. I always felt that these categories are way too simplistic. It's also my belief that there is a tendency in American society to victimize individuals of different backgrounds. While the intention of identifying minorities is commendable, it risks leaving people with fewer possibilities for empowerment.

Years ago, while doing my master's and studying Cook-Greuter's Ego Development Theory[16], I couldn't help but identify myself with many aspects of the Individualist Stage. Cook-Greuter (p. 55) states that people at this stage of development tend to "reevaluate the soundness of the prefixed role identities that society offers and sanctions. One must redefine themselves uniquely and independently of these givens based on their own experience, values, and conclusions." *Bang!* That's it. This feeling of being put in one box defined by someone who has no idea who I am is what bothers me. Not just being in a box, but being forced by others into boxes. Why do people always have to say who I am when they have no idea who I really am? So, I am who I am. I am Latina, Brazilian, of Iberian origin, who immigrated to the US seeking an adventure while building my career and developing myself. In which box does that fit?

---

[16] Cook-Greuter, S. (2013). Nine levels of increasing embrace in ego development: A full-spectrum theory of vertical development and meaning-making. Wayland, MA: Cook-Greuter & Associates.

9

AN OPTIMIST WITH A PLAN B

---∞---

Optimism is the belief that the odds of a good outcome are in your favor over time, even when there will be setbacks along the way.

-Morgan Housel

Years ago, during an HR team offsite, we were asked to take a personality test called Enneagram. Although I have a Psychology degree and have studied many personality instruments, until that point, I was not very familiar with this one. But I was curious. What would this test tell me that I don't already know?

After completing the assessment, I had a debrief session with the offsite facilitator to understand its results. It turns out I am that optimistic person who always has a plan B. I am hopeful things will work out the way I want, but my self-preservation subtype is always whispering in my ears, "What if this is not meant to be?"

As I continued to read the description assigned to my Enneagram 7 Self-Preservation, things were making a lot of sense and shedding light on how I think and how I behave.

The type 7 in me loves to brainstorm new ideas all the time, sees the positive side even during bad times, and enjoys the freedom of unlimited possibilities. But the self-preservation instinct is attuned to having the most basic survival resources, including food, shelter, and safety. It's an interesting balance.

That has been true to me for most of my life. I remember when I was at the US Consulate in São Paulo, standing in line to get my J-1 visa to join the Au Pair in America program, while also planning all the things I could do if my visa was denied. My university had a partnership with the *Universidad de Santiago de Compostela*, in Spain, and as I was waiting for hours in a long line to be interviewed by a US consular officer, I was generating a lot of ideas and started getting excited about this new possibility. It will be great to learn Spanish and travel through Spain and the rest of Europe. Oh, all the things I could do and places I could go! The Enneagram 7 tends to avoid pain, and generating new ideas is a coping mechanism to escape those negative emotions.

As I am writing these words, I am going through one of the most interesting moments of my career. The company I work for filed for Chapter 11, aka bankruptcy, and my Enneagram 7 Self-Preservation is in full swing. While the filing itself brought me a new wave of hope for a better future for the company, the Self-Preservation subtype makes me feel uneasy. I want to stay there and be part of a successful story (the Optimist/Visionary side of me), but at the same time, I am considering all the ideas I have about not being there anymore (the Self-Preservation side) in case the company cannot successfully emerge from bankruptcy.

Beatrice Chestnut, PhD, describes the Seven Self-Preservation type as having a tendency "to always have their nose to the wind to sniff out good opportunities"[17] (p.233). I am thinking about having a coaching practice, I am researching how to open an LLC in California, I am thinking about interviewing for new jobs as a Chief People Officer for start-ups or going back two steps in my career and have a less challenging but stable job at a larger organization. *Less challenging job? Fewer opportunities to brainstorm new ideas and be creative? Who am I kidding? We all know I would be bored in six months!*

---

[17] Chestnut, B. (2017). 9 types of leadership: Mastering the art of people in the 21st Century workplace. Post Hill Press.

I believe that the lesson here is not to have all answers but to be open to considering things that might be seen as peculiar in other people's eyes.

10

ALL YOU NEED IS LOVE

∞

Happiness should not, must not, can never be a goal, but only an outcome.

-Viktor Frankl

There is no non-stop flight from San Francisco to São Paulo. It takes nearly an entire day to travel to Brazil, including going to/from the airport, flight times, and layovers. My biggest fear after I moved to the US was that if anything bad would happen to my family, I would be unable to immediately be there for them.

For the first several years, while I was adapting to my new life, the "universe" was generous to me; nothing that I was fearful of ever happened, and I was able to visit my family annually during my favorite season: Christmas and New Year's.

Christmas has always been a lot of fun with my family. Until we were in our teens, my siblings and I didn't have any first cousins, so our uncles and aunts spoiled us quite a bit and always gifted us with shiny new toys and visits to amusement parks and theaters.

For starters, Christmas is in the summertime in Brazil. Despite what all the American movies show us, I still prefer to hope for a little breeze on Christmas Eve to cool us down instead of having a white Christmas in the Northern Hemisphere. The warmth of the weather reflects on people's moods and approach to one another. The evening of Christmas Eve is "the big event." The entire family gets together. We are loud, and we talk over each other. Even after my parents separated when I was a teenager and my dad moved to another state, he would always come home for Christmas and eventually started bringing my new siblings over as well. So, there have always been new generations of kids at our Christmas parties, and I love seeing the magic in children's eyes receiving their gifts.

Maybe it's just me projecting my own childhood. It was always the most special time of the year.

Fast forward after moving to San Francisco, I always had great expectations around the holidays so I could go back home, see my family, celebrate Christmas, and do our Secret Santa gift exchange.

Then, a few years later, in November of 2014, I was engaged and about to get married in the San Francisco City Hall. Two days before flying to San Francisco for my wedding, my mom received the diagnosis that would literally change her life. It was that c-word that we don't want to think about and don't want to talk about, as if the f-ing cancer would disappear if we were in denial.

By March of 2015, when we were having the Brazilian wedding ceremony, my mom was already in chemotherapy. She had lost her hair and found a beautiful wig that matched her style so much that no one could tell it was not her natural hair. The day of my wedding was raining dogs and cats in São Paulo, the famous waters of March closing out the summer[18]. Despite Alanis Morrisette's lyrics of Ironic, they say in Brazil that raining on your wedding day is good luck. I was getting a little nervous with all that rain and became a bridezilla for a moment. But as soon as we arrived at the salon where we would get ready, my mood changed. My mom, my sister, my sister-in-law, and my best friends were there. We were drinking champagne, talking, laughing, and getting pampered. What is not to like? My

---

[18] Reference to Tom Jobim's famous bossa-nova song, Águas de Março.

mom looked gorgeous. Seriously. I was just enjoying every second of this girls-get-together.

Even though I was officially married already, having all our families and friends together in one of the most iconic places in São Paulo was awe-inspiring. It was a beautiful ceremony at the rooftop restaurant of the tallest building in São Paulo. It was a joyful celebration and we all had great wine and amazing food cooked by an authentic five-star Italian chef, and we danced the entire night to our favorite songs.

My mom was very brave and strong, and I was hopeful she would fight with all her strengths. And she did. But after a little over a year of remission, the cancer had come back and metastasized. And there I was, booking last-minute trips to São Paulo so I could be with her. I am grateful that I could financially afford it and was able to take the time off to be there. But every time, I could see that her health was deteriorating and there was no turning point anymore.

When I was approached on LinkedIn by a new company, I was excited because this new role offered nearly everything that was important to me. But I was a little hesitant; there was that voice inside me, "What if something happens? And you are in a new job, you need to prove yourself, and you won't be able to take time off?" I shook it off and, still a little bit in denial, thinking my mom still had at least another year or so.

However, my mom's hospital visits were becoming more frequent. In early 2018, I was there with her in the hospital.

Once she was ready to go home, I was ready to fly back to San Francisco and start my new job.

One week after my start date, I was sitting in my new office and getting my workday started when I got a call from my sister. "Dr. Marcelo said it's time for you to come home." It felt like my world collapsed. The next day, my husband and I were boarding the first flight to Brazil, and for the next two weeks, we watched my mom slowly dying in the ICU.

She was in an induced coma, but I was there every day with her. I played Dancing Queen on my phone and danced, holding her hands. Until one day, the nurse entered the room and caught us! I was a little embarrassed, but she was laughing and encouraged me, "Don't stop; this is good for her." And those were my days and nights in an ICU room with my mom, playing our favorite songs with the unstoppable beeps of all those machines keeping her alive in the background. I thought I was going a little crazy.

When we flew to São Paulo, my mother-in-law sent me a beautiful message saying that the most important thing for a mom is to know their children will be okay, so even though my mom was in an induced coma, I should tell her that we would be fine. Every day, I was with my mom in the ICU; some nights, I slept there, and sometimes, I went back home. But every day, I would say, "See you tomorrow." The doctor had talked to me one day, saying there was really nothing else that could be done, and it was now a matter of time, so we should prepare to say goodbye. I couldn't. The following days, when I left the ICU room, I would still say, "See you tomorrow." But one day, I had the courage to say, "If you are tired of staying here, it is okay. We will be fine, and we will take care of each other." That day, I didn't say "See you tomorrow."

At 4:30 am, I got a call from the hospital saying the doctor requested our presence. We knew what that meant. I then missed holding her hands in that ICU room. During our last goodbye to her, we sat there holding hands while listening to All You Need is Love.

"Nothing prepared me for the loss of my mother. Even knowing that she would die did not prepare me. A mother, after all, is your entry to the world. She is the shell in which you divide and become a life. Waking up in a world without her is like waking up in a world without sky: unimaginable" – Meghan O'Rourke

After she passed, my number one concern was my grandma. She had already lost my uncle years before. She did not deserve to lose another child. For me, my grandma was the life of the party. She defined "laughing out loud." She was the right balance between being funny and feisty. Maybe I got that from her. When I was a kid, my mom decided to go back to work. So, we stayed with a maid at home who took us to school, and then my mom would pick us up. But sometimes, we would stay with my grandma (in between firing a housekeeper and finding a new one). And I loved staying there. Allegedly, I had a lot of headaches, and sometimes I even wondered how bad these headaches really were, but they were enough for me to call my mom and ask if I could skip school that day.

I spent so many afternoons with my grandma. My grandma used to make these little cakes called *bolinho de chuva*, which is something similar to a donut hole, that I absolutely loved. There was another version of that recipe, where she deep-fried the dough in a small ring format and then quickly dipped it in *pinga* and sprinkled it with sugar. This was called *Rosquinha de Pinga*. *Pinga* is another word for cachaça, which is a sort of rum made from sugar cane. Very healthy for an 8-year-old, huh?

But what I always loved about watching my grandma cook was that she never followed any recipe. She had all the steps and ingredients memorized, and as she was explaining what she was doing, she would always say, "You put a little more of this, and you will know when it's good." How do you know, you might ask. "You will know." In fact, after my mom passed, I kept her recipe book. In a Julie & Julia style, I was inspired to cook every recipe in the book to honor her memory. After a few tries, I realized my mom's recipe book was just like my grandma's cooking style. It feels like every recipe is missing some important step, but you will know when it's right. And that's how I honor them both. I love to cook, but I don't follow any recipes. I research, read many different recipes, and then get inspired with whatever I have in my pantry. My husband says I *patify* the recipes (in reference to my nickname, Pati). And that's a compliment for those who are wondering.

So, the following year, after my mom had passed, there I was, jumping on the next flight to Brazil again. I wanted to see my grandma alive for the last time. I did. She was in the hospital. The day I saw her, she was awake and lucid, but we all knew she was departing. She was holding very strong. And finally, she passed peacefully in her sleep a few days after I flew back home.

Shortly after that, in early 2020, as we all know now, the world stopped. I was lucky enough to be getting information about Covid early on. I had two colleagues in China who were sharing with me what was going on there. So, I knew it was a matter of when, not if, Covid would hit us. At work, I became part of a newly-created Covid Task Force. While many companies started implementing work-from-home policies in early March, my company had a CEO who was reluctant to send people to work remotely. We would frequently hear, "We are not there yet." But we kept hearing about other companies that had to completely shut down because of confirmed Covid cases in their facilities.

Even though everyone was talking about Covid, it took a lot of work to get reliable information. What is this? Who is at risk? What is really happening? I was naïve to think humans would fight this together and if the world shut down for a couple of months, Covid would go away. Well, we now know how that went.

In the early days of Covid, I felt a sense of responsibility that maybe only parents feel. I was so afraid someone at work would catch Covid in the office, go home, spread it to their families, and their loved ones would die. That was the story that repeatedly kept playing in my head. Not only was I worried about business continuity and finding a solution to help the company not lose millions of dollars, but I couldn't help myself and think about all those families that could be at risk if we didn't send people to work remotely right now! Maybe it was my own grieving process. I had just lost my mom and my grandma, and I wanted to protect people to not feel what I felt.

Finally, the CEO allowed people to work remotely, and most of us in Corporate America saw our ways of working evolve dramatically right before our eyes. In March 2020, I wrote this piece for a school paper:

The Path Forward

There are still a lot of uncertainties about the future. No one knows for sure how long this pandemic will last. California is currently under a Shelter in Place order. It has been three weeks since we created the task-force, and, as of March 22, 2020, there are over 38,000 confirmed cases in the USA[19] (Worldometer, 2020). It has been nearly a week since the organization activated stage 3 of the pandemic plan, which means, all employees have to work from home unless they are considered necessary to maintain "minimum basic operations", per the Alameda County Shelter in Place order[20] (Health Officer of the Alameda County, 2020). However, not even the county authorities could specify what "minimum basic operations" mean, and the organization's leaders are now trying to define which laboratory work can be done during the Shelter in Place and how to go back to work when the Shelter in Place order is lifted.

---

[19] Worldometer (2020). Covid-19 Coronavirus Pandemic. https://www.worldometers.info/coronavirus/country/us/
[20] Health Officer of the Alameda County. (2020, March 16). Final Order to Shelter at Home. http://www.acgov.org/documents/Final-Order-to-Shelter-In-Place.pdf

The impact of this health crisis is already substantial, and it will have a long-lasting impact on how we organize our work. The experience of participating in this task-force has been one of the most challenging moments in my career (if not the most challenging), and I continue to learn how to influence leaders, how to strategize in the middle of the chaos, and how to effectively communicate inside and outside of the task-force.

When I look into the future, there are mixed feelings of hope and despair. How can humanity get out of this crisis and create a more sustainable future when we still have leaders in our organizations and nations who are focusing more on the economic losses instead of the impact on people's lives. Mohrman & Shani (2011) argue that successfully addressing challenges like this "entails intentionally altering the patterns of interaction and activities in our complex system in which all of our activities have economic, societal and environmental impacts" (p. 8).

During the last few weeks, despite the difficulties the task-force has encountered, I have seen a lot of positive reactions, from leaders stepping up to contain the spread of the virus to the broader community helping each other. As humanity faces this challenge together, there is an opportunity to alter the way we live and work to create a more sustainable future.

As I wrote that piece, that sense of despair was already taking place. I was one of those individuals who would rarely leave the house, order food and groceries online to avoid any public space, sanitize every single object that entered my house, and work very long hours, trying to determine my workspace and personal space.

I was anxious to get over the pandemic but saw early on that we were not all on the same page. While I am proud that everyone in my family took this seriously and took steps to prevent illness, by the summer of 2020, my family was also impacted. My grandpa was infected by Covid in his nursing home, and what initially seemed like "just a cold" ended up taking his life.

That time, I couldn't jump on the first flight back to Brazil to be with my family. My grandpa, who was a Portuguese immigrant, worked very hard his entire life to provide a better future for his family. But he didn't have the dignity of having a funeral. Due to the contagious nature of the virus, his body was put in a plastic bag and sent straight to the cemetery where he was buried. No one could hug. For the first time since I moved to the US, I didn't go home for the holidays.

At the beginning of the pandemic, I lived in a small house and didn't have a dedicated space to work. So, early on, I bought a small desk, put it in a corner of the living room, and called it "my corner office." The view was gorgeous, but the space was too small to live and work, and I was tired of feeling restricted.

In the following several months and throughout the year 2021, I was thriving at work and school. I completed an Executive Development Program, finished a Master's program, and got a promotion. Everything was going well. But I was burned out.

Even though I was getting better at setting boundaries between work and personal life, the Covid Task Force at work demanded 24/7 attention. I was the one doing contact tracing and making phone calls, sometimes late at night, so impacted people could take immediate action.

By early 2022, after taking all Covid vaccine shots, including a booster, I was sensing this feeling of normalcy coming back to the world. I don't typically make New Year's Resolutions, but that time, I decided that my goal in 2022 would be to do one different thing per month. That could be anything small, like a hike or a picnic, or something major, like a vacation in French Polynesia. January: spent a weekend at Universal Studios Hollywood. February: a long weekend in Seattle. March/April: I went to Brazil for the birth of my wonderful niece, Manuela. May: the dream vacation in Tahiti and Bora Bora. June: spent my birthday paddle boarding in Lodi followed by wine tasting.

That first half of the year was going well, but I forgot to mention to the "Universe" that my real intention was to do something different and good once a month. When I woke up on July 6, there were lots of WhatsApp messages, including one from my sister: "Call me as soon as you wake up."

Obviously, that didn't seem right. But I would never have guessed that it was my dad's time to depart. He had a heart attack shortly after waking up that day. From that moment, I felt my head was spinning. And here we go again. We had just a couple of hours to book flights, hotel, pack, and leave for the airport.

The next day, we arrived in Brazil to see my dad for the very last time. My head is still spinning. Of course it is; I've been crying for the last 24 hours, took 3 different flights to arrive in Curitiba, and barely slept on the plane. A day later, I went with all my family to my dad's favorite restaurant. It was special to be there, eating some of his favorite food and honoring his memory.

Two days later, my head is still spinning, and now I have chills and a scratchy throat. I was no longer a "NOvid". That lingering headache I had was Covid, and I was stuck with my husband in a tiny Airbnb in Brazil for the following two weeks.

Growing up, whenever I was not feeling well, I would just ask my mom to make "my soup." My soup is a mix of veggies and meat that my mom blended in the mixer so well, reaching the consistency of a bisque. But now, I don't have either of my parents to make my wishes come true and spoil me. (side note: my dad's wife was very sweet in her attempt to make "my soup." It was not exactly like my mom's – of course not – but it was very good for this Covid patient.)

Weeks and months went by. It's impossible not to think about my parents every single day. But as I grieved on my own time, I can think about them nowadays with joy and love and a little less sadness. They've always done the best they could with what they knew at the time. They were Winnicott's[21] description of good enough parents. And I am

---

[21] Donald Winnicott was a psychoanalyst who coined the term "good enough mother" in 1953, after observing hundreds of babies and their moms. A good enough mother is loving and attentive, but is not perfect, allowing room for the child's independence and autonomy.

grateful because they taught me to be kind but strong; caring but independent.

The following year, I updated my New Year's resolution to "do one *fun* thing per month." It worked out. Even as my company went through Chapter 11 bankruptcy restructuring and my work became increasingly challenging, I was able to find the time, the energy, and joy to do things I love, helping me to keep my sanity.

A while ago, I heard someone saying (I wish I knew who said that to properly give credit to them), "Resilience is like a savings account; the more you use it, the more you have it." Life just keeps proving that.

My mantra now is "I will do the best I can with what I've got." And as Rita Lee[22] beautifully said, "Everything is all right. Even what is wrong, it's all right."

---

[22] Rita Lee was an inspiring singer and composer, and famous "Queen of Rock" in Brazil. The sentence I quote here is from her second memoir, which she wrote during the years of 2021 and 2022 as she was battling cancer. The book was published in May 2023, shortly after her passing.

EPILOGUE

When I was maybe in 5th or 6th grade, I was starting to build the habit of reading newspapers. I always heard everyone around me talking about how important it was to read the news and be informed about everything. So, I wanted to be part of that in-group. I never really liked the scent and the texture of newspaper material, which made me sneeze each time I turned the pages. Still, I felt this was an important practice, so I carried on.

Then, one day, a family member (who I love dearly but shall remain unnamed here) asked me the fatidic question every grown-up asks a child, "what are you going to be when you grow up?" I thought I wanted to be a journalist, and she asked me back in a slightly judgmental tone, "A journalist?! But are you good at writing?" I responded, "No," and shut this idea down. I never again thought of being a journalist.

I don't know whether I was good at writing. But if I knew then what I know now, my answer would be, "I am probably not very good yet; I am only in 5th grade. But if I keep practicing, I can be really good at this. And excuse me, I will go back to my newspaper here." Obviously, this would have been a more sophisticated thought process for a fifth grader who knew nothing about Growth Mindset and had no idea who Carol Dweck was.

But the point is that many of these interactions we have at a young age shape who we are and how confident we are with our own abilities. What I described above is not to blame this one family member but to highlight this outdated belief that you need to be naturally good at certain things to be able to succeed.

It was only when I went to university that I started feeling more confident about my writing skills. I had to read a lot and write many client reports and papers. Over time, I knew I was writing better than ever before.

Years later, I moved to the US, and you can imagine by now what happened. Writing in my second language was challenging, and all that insecurity from my youth came right back. It was as if my insecurity was always there, trying to find opportunities to show up again.

I don't have a background in internal communications, but this is an area that I used to do fairly well when writing in Portuguese. But at my jobs in the US, I was always nervous about hitting the "send" button. I checked what I had written many times and sometimes would *google* the expressions I wrote just to make sure someone else in the world of the internet also wrote that way. I had this constant feeling of being a fraud and someone would find out that everything I wrote was wrong and worthless.

Despite being a lifelong learner who was always "itching" to go back to school, I felt intimidated by graduate-level writing in English. At some point, I took a leap of faith and enrolled in the Evidence-Based Coaching certificate program, followed by the Master's degree in Organizational Development and Leadership a couple of years later. By then, I had started to feel better about my writing capabilities. I think it was around this time that I started to feel that those two personalities, Brazilian and American, started to merge. Being able to communicate nearly the same way in either language is much more than knowing vocabulary and grammar. It's about choosing the right words, tone, and timing.

In part, I believe that the process of writing this book is a little bit of self-healing. The creative process of writing helps to unravel our deeper questions and dilemmas so we can resolve them and move on.

As I complete this project, I know the work is not completed. And I hope it never is. As long as I live, I aspire to remain receptive to all lessons awaiting to be learned. And my faith in the world is that everyone has the capability and the opportunity to learn and move on.

ABOUT THE AUTHOR

Patricia East is a global HR Executive and Leadership Coach. Over a decade ago, Patricia embarked on a transformative journey, relocating from Brazil to the United States, where she rebuilt an HR career in innovative technology and biotechnology companies. She has a degree in Psychology, graduate certificates in Business Administration, Evidence-Based Coaching, and a master's degree in Organizational Development and Leadership. Her first book, *Passport to Growth: Leadership Lessons from an Expat*, is an introspection about her journey from her early years of life up to her career to become a successful HR leader in a new country.

www.ingramcontent.com/pod-product-compliance
Lightning Source LLC
Chambersburg PA
CBHW032004060526
44119CB00109B/43